Becoming a Father: What New Dads Should Expect & 99 Baby Tips to Survive Your Newborn's First Three Months

By: Clayton Geoffreys

Copyright © 2015 by Clayton Geoffreys

All rights reserved. Neither this book nor any portion thereof may be reproduced or used in any manner whatsoever without the express written permission. Published in the United States of America.

Disclaimer: The following book is for entertainment and informational purposes only. The information presented is without contract or any type of guarantee assurance. While every caution has been taken to provide accurate and current information, it is solely the reader's responsibility to check all information contained in this article before relying upon it. Neither the author nor publisher can be held accountable for any errors or omissions. Under no circumstances will any legal responsibility or blame be held against the author or publisher for any reparation, damages, or monetary loss due to the information presented, either directly or indirectly. This book is not intended as legal or medical advice. If any such specialized advice is needed, seek a qualified individual for help.

Trademarks are used without permission. Use of the trademark is not authorized by, associated with, or sponsored by the trademark owners. All trademarks and brands used within this book are used with no intent to infringe on the trademark owners and only used for clarifying purposes.

Visit my website at www.claytongeoffreys.com

Cover photo by Keith Allison is licensed under CC BY 2.0 / modified from original

Table of Contents

Foreword 1

Introduction 4

Chapter 1: Month One – What to Expect 5

   Month One: Tips & Tricks 10

      Baby Basics 10

      You, Her & Them 23

      Gear & Supplies 32

Chapter Two: Month Two – What to Expect 43

   Month Two: Tips & Tricks 47

      Baby Basics 47

      You, Her & Them 57

      Gear & Supplies 63

   Month Three: Tips & Tricks 80

      Baby Basics 80

You, Her & Them	91
Gear & Supplies	99
Conclusion	108
Final Word/About the Author	109
Endnotes	110

Foreword

When my first son, Christopher, was born, it was an incredible day for me. I vividly remember the first time I held Christopher in my arms. It was magical. To me, that moment defined and fundamentally changed my life. I was a new dad. And needless to say, I was scared. Leading up to the big day, I read up on many books to prepare for Christopher's birth, but something I felt was lacking was a book that helped detail what to do the first three months when your newborn has just settled into your home. This is why I was inspired to write this book. I get it. Being a new dad is a **huge** change and in many ways, you feel as though you do not know what in the world you are doing. That is okay. I promise you, that while the next three months will be busy, they will be incredibly rewarding as you begin raising your newborn child and nurturing him or her with your love. Hopefully from reading *Becoming a Father: What New Dads Should Expect & 99 Baby*

Tips to Survive Your Newborn's First Three Months, I can help you quell your concerns on what to expect in months one through three, while also providing you with tons of key tips for caring for your newborn. These are the lessons that I learned the hard way but hopefully after reading this book, you will not experience so many surprises as I did. Thank you for downloading my book. Hope you enjoy and if you do, please do not forget to leave a review! Also, check out my website at claytongeoffreys.com to join my exclusive list where I let you know about my latest books. To thank you for your purchase, you can go there to download a free copy of *33 Life Lessons: Success Principles, Career Advice & Habits of Successful People*. In the book, you'll learn from greatest thought leaders of on what it takes to become successful and how to live a great life.

Cheers,

Clayton Geoffreys

Visit me at www.claytongeoffreys.com

Introduction

Congratulations! You are now a dad. You have entered a new and exciting world that is both difficult and highly rewarding. You can look forward to exhausting nights and stressful days, but with a little information to guide you, the confusion and frustration of these crazy days can be significantly reduced. In this article, we will discuss your new baby's first three months. We'll cover basic information about your infant's development and needs in each month, followed by a quick list of tips and hints that will, hopefully, make these first weeks easier and more rewarding.

Chapter 1: Month One – What to Expect[1]

Month one began very dramatically for your new little bundle. Birth was difficult, not just for your baby's mother, but for the baby, too! Her transition from a warm, quiet, comfortable existence into our loud, bright, and crazy world was exciting and exhausting, and now that you have brought her home, she has a lot of hard work to do adjusting to her new environment.

At this stage your baby has two priorities: eat and sleep. Newborns can sleep 16-17 hours a day, and for the first few days, she will wake up only to eat. She will eat every 2-3 hours, and this is normal, though you should not expect an exact schedule. And keep in mind that a baby cannot be spoiled at this stage, so it's fine to attend to her immediately when she does wake up.

Also remember that these earliest feedings can take 30-45 minutes at a time. While sucking is a natural reflex (try sticking your pinkie finger into your baby's mouth to find out just how strong that reflex is), she has never had to feed herself before now. Without the umbilical cord she now has to learn how to coordinate all of the muscles in her body to get food into her belly. If you have a champion latcher, great, but for most babies, learning to latch correctly takes a lot of work. Another eating issue that can arise at this stage is a lazy eater. Some babies simply don't have the stamina to continue sucking until they are full. They can doze off, ending the feeding early. This may result in low milk supply for mom and a need to supplement with formula, but eventually even lazy eaters can get the hang of the whole eating "thing." Lastly, if mom is breastfeeding, both of them are learning a new skill, so both mom and baby need time to practice. Within a few weeks, feedings will start to go much faster, which will help everyone get much-needed sleep.

Many changes that your baby will experience in these first few weeks are physical. Some of them are strange, but are not serious issues.[2] For example, a baby's skull is not fused when she is born, so she will have soft spots on her head called fontanels. These can be confusing, even weird (they can pulse with the baby's heartbeat), but they are not dangerous. You can touch them, gently of course, because a membrane protects the baby's brain until they close completely (by four months in the rear, and one year in the front). Another physical reality is the umbilical cord. If you cut it in the delivery room, great work! Unfortunately, the stump has to be properly attended until it falls off in a few days. While you wait for that major milestone, make sure to keep the area dry and unencumbered. Many newborn diapers even have a front notch to keep the diaper from rubbing on the cord stump (if not, you can fold down the front side of the diaper to prevent irritation). And you and mom will want to give only sponge baths until the cord is completely gone.

One final thought about the physical reality of your newborn: keep in mind that a newborn baby can be...well...less than picturesque. Some are covered in a fine hair (called lanugo) that falls off in the first few weeks. Others have a wrinkled appearance, and many look more like a miniature senior citizen than a newborn. Some babies have less control of their eye muscles and seem to be cross-eyed most of the time. All of this is normal, and you can be assured that in a matter of days, your baby will take on the round, "normal" appearance of a picture-perfect baby.[3]

However, physical changes are only part of your little bundle's story. At first, of course, your newborn is not specifically attached to you, but quickly; she will recognize your smell and voice. Bonding is an individual thing. It takes time, but it will happen.

While the first few days will be a blur of feedings, diaper changes, and parental uncertainty, your new family unit will start to come together. You will start to recognize that your baby's cries mean different things. You will begin to see her respond in different ways, especially if she is tired or over stimulated. Mentally and emotionally, she needs lots of attention for these first weeks. Talk to her, hold her when she's awake and asleep, sing to her, massage her gently and carry her with you as you go about your day. These activities prepare her for the bonding and emotional maturity that each new stage will bring.

By the end of her first month, your baby has gathered an immense amount of information through her senses. She will be learning all the time. She will be interacting more with you, fixing her eyes on you and moving her face as if she's talking (she's not really controlling her face yet, but it's a good way to interact with her). Your baby will be starting to show a bit of personality, and you will start to see some of your hard work pay off. Of course, there is still a great deal of work to do in the coming months, but Month One is an exciting and rewarding beginning.

Month One: Tips & Tricks

<u>Baby Basics</u>

1. Input/Output

At this point, your little one will **do** almost nothing. But she will do *a lot* of it. I'm referring, of course, to pee and poop. Here is a quick run-down of the basics.

- All babies poop. If yours isn't, you need to call the doctor – yesterday.
  Babies will not poop on schedule yet, but they need to be changed regularly.
  Tying diaper changes to each feeding, even at night, is a great way to remember.
- It is important to keep track of your baby's output, especially for the first few days. You can

use a variety of apps, charts or plain old scrap paper, but the list will reveal how well she's eating or whether she's dehydrated. If you aren't sure, call the pediatrician's on-call nurse and check.

2. **Poop Progression & Potency**[4]

- Stage 1 – Meconium looks like motor oil and sticks like caramel to the entire diapered region. It's made up of all the stuff your baby "took in" before she was born – amniotic fluid, skin cells, and other such substances. It comes first, is very hard to clean off, but rarely smells at all.
- Stage 2 – Early poop. This stage of poop is usually a greenish color and lasts for much of the first week of life.
- Stage 3a – Breastfed poop. The breastfed baby's poop can be a range of colors (yellow or greenish usually), and it may have what looks like cottage cheese or small seeds in it. It will be

creamier and easier to clean than the meconium. There can be lots of volume at this stage but overall, very little smell.

- Stage 3b – Formula poop. A bottle-fed baby generally poops a brown color (tan to mocha) and a thicker, creamy consistency. If you use an iron-fortified formula, the poop can sometimes be dark brown or dark green. This does not happen often, but it is fine.
- Stage 4+ - Once your child starts eating real food (cereal, baby food, etc.), she will start to poop "real" poop that will look and smell pretty much like what you produce.

3. **Diapering: A Quick How-To**[5]

- Gather all supplies first. Grab a new diaper, wipes and diaper rash cream, just in case.
- Lay baby carefully face up on the floor or changing table.

- Remove or tuck out of the way any clothes that will interfere with your mission.
- Remove used diaper and set aside or quickly roll into a poop burrito and seal with tabs.
- Open the new diaper and lay it just below the baby's behind.
- Grab both ankles with one hand and lift the baby's rear end gently. Slide the fresh diaper into place before lowering her hips.
- Pull the diaper between baby's legs and secure with tabs.
- Reclothe the baby and lay her in a safe location (off the changing table).
- Discard the diaper. Wash your hands. Mission complete!

4. Diaper Duty: Tips and Reminders

- Gather your supplies before you start. Every time. (I know, I repeated that from above, but one day you will thank me for it.)
- Wipe all the cracks and crevices carefully. Keeping baby's bottom clean will help prevent serious diaper rash. So clean and clean again! Also, wipe little girls from front to back to keep from spreading germs into her most sensitive parts.[6]
- Every baby will, at some point, pee or poop on you while being changed – even girls (it simply goes OUT, not UP). Always be ready to clean up a puddle when a diaper is off.

5. Diaper Duty: Notes on Boys

- Thar he blows! You do not need PeePee-TeePees or similar "tents" to protect from spraying, but cool air on a little penis can result in a small fountain, so just be prepared. Keep a cloth handy to cover the flow and be ready with a change of clothes for him (and possibly yourself).

- Other news. Your mantra should be, "Shooter down!" Always point his penis down, into the diaper, as you fold it up. Leaving it aimed at the waistline will mean more leaks.
- Take care to properly attend a circumcised penis. Follow your pediatrician's directions carefully to avoid infections.

6. Just like You Cradle the Football (or the Video Game Remote)

- You will quickly become a master of holding your new little baby, but until its second nature, just remember a couple of things.
- Her head is your responsibility. She cannot hold it up by herself, so you must support it for her.

- Turn your hand diagonally so that your index finger is the highest point. Put that fingertip at the crown of her head, and use your thumb and pinkie finger to support near the ears. The butt of your palm will rest at the base of her skull for full support.
- She is breakable, but not easily broken. Simply be careful when you pick her up or move her. You will quickly learn a variety of ways that she does (and does not) enjoy being held.

7. Papa Kangaroo

Kangaroo Kare means holding your baby skin-to-skin. The nurses at the hospital probably encouraged your baby's mom, and maybe even you, to do it. But it is important to continue skin-to-skin contact when you get home. Hold the baby, undressed but covered with a blanket, against your bare chest. She will love it, and it will help you bond with your new little one.

8. Soothing Secrets

Here are a few starter ideas for your soothing arsenal. They can be used alone or together, and they are some of the most effective options for calming an unhappy baby.

- <u>Shushing</u>. This means exactly what it sounds like. Gently and quietly "sh sh-sh" to your baby as you snuggle or rock her. The sound is a helpful one that can work quickly to calm and quiet your little one.
- <u>Swaying</u>. Before she was born, her mom rocked your little girl back and forth constantly. Now that she is out in the bright, loud world, you can help her feel that kind of safety again by mimicking that rocking, swaying motion.
- <u>Singing</u>. You don't have to be Frank Sinatra or Michael Bublé to soothe your baby with song. Keep it simple and quiet. You can even hum.

But the rhythm of the music and your calm voice will help quiet and relax her.
- <u>Shifting the Mood</u>. Darken the lights. Pull down the shades. Take the baby to a quiet room.

9. SIDS[7]

Sudden Infant Death Syndrome is the leading cause of death in children 1 month to 1 year old. There is no absolute way to prevent SIDS, but you *can* reduce your child's risk.

- ALWAYS put your baby to sleep on her back. **Always**.
- Avoid thick bumpers and blankets in the crib (swaddling will keep your baby warm).
- Avoid overheating the baby with too-heavy clothes or too many coverings.
- Keep the baby away from cigarette smoke.
- Breastfeeding and sleeping in the same room both seem to reduce the risk of SIDS.

- Use a pacifier when you put the baby to sleep.

10. Boobs or Bottles?

- A feeding cycle is counted from the beginning of one feeding to the beginning of the next. So no matter how long it takes the baby to eat, you will need to feed her 2-3 hours after she *starts* eating each time.
- Breastfeeding means giving the baby breast milk to drink, whether directly from the breast or from bottles. There are three types of breast milk.[8]
  - ☐ Colostrum: the first milk produced by a mother's breast. It provides nutrients until mom's actual milk comes in.
  - ☐ Fore milk: the first milk released when a baby starts each feeding. It is lower in calories, so if your baby seems to be hungry very soon after nursing, encourage her to eat longer and get more of the hind milk, too.

- ☐ Hind milk: the most nutrient-rich milk. It is high in calories and fills the baby for longer. Getting enough hind milk will result in a "milk drunk" look of contentment.
- Breastfeeding has many benefits. It costs next to nothing to do. A mother's body adjusts her milk to the baby's needs. As she needs more, she produces more. As the baby gets older, the breast milk changes, too. Lastly, breast milk provides immunity for the baby from a variety of sicknesses.[9]
- The other feeding option is formula. Created to mimic breast milk, formula is designed to meet a multitude of nutritional and allergy-related needs. It is an effective food for your baby, and bottle-feeding is an excellent alternative for those who choose it.
- The benefits of formula are also numerous. Using formula means that anyone can feed the

baby at any time, which can help reduce stress for the mother. It is easily portable; making it helpful for mothers who must return to work soon after the baby is born. Formula-fed babies are every bit as healthy as nursing babies, so it is a safe and effective feeding alternative.

- There will, of course, be a lot of pressure on your baby's mom about which option she chooses. Do your best to support whatever decision she makes.

11. Baby Burritos: How to Swaddle

- Lay a blanket down in a diamond shape.
- Fold down the top corner to the diamond's center to create a flat side. Lay the baby so her shoulders are at the flat edge.
- Bring the bottom corner up and tuck it over the baby's body.
- Bring one of the sides across the infant, tucking the corner securely under the baby's body.

- Wrap the final corner around the baby to create the swaddle shape.
- Reminder: Keep the swaddle firm but not too tight. Practice will make perfect, and it won't be long before you can make a perfect baby "burrito."

12. Survival Secrets

Where should you go for ideas and information about managing the crazy world of newborns?

- Family & friends are always willing to listen and give advice.
- You can always call your baby's pediatrician and office staff (especially the on-call nurse).
- Websites such as babycenter.com, parents.com or whattoexpect.com provide lots of information as well as ideas that other parents have submitted. You can also join a "birth month club," allowing you to network with other families in a similar stage of life.

13. Month One Checkups

Your baby will have a well visit at the pediatrician's office at one week old and one month old. Nurses will record the baby's height and weight. The doctor will ask questions about the baby's general behavior. You can ask questions, too. It's good to write down your questions ahead of time to make the appointment flow smoothly. Generally you should leave these appointments feeling well supported to manage the task of parenting until the next time you arrive.

You, Her & Them

14. Pet Patrol

Do your best to prepare your pet before the new baby's arrival. Once your baby is born, allow your pet plenty of opportunity to see, smell and interact with your child, all with sufficient supervision. A baby in utero can hear what is going on outside her cozy world, so if your dog has barked at the doorbell for the entire pregnancy, it will be a familiar (though much louder) sound now. Watch for allergic reactions in the baby, and if you are concerned about your pet's behavior, contact a professional trainer.[10]

15. Momma Maintenance – Recovery & Pain Support

Your baby's mom has recently endured one of the most painful and physically challenging trials of her life. Whether she had an epidural, a natural birth, or a C-section, you can help her recover in a number of specific ways.

- Vaginal deliveries (natural or medicated) will keep your baby's mother from moving easily. She will (and should) spend a lot of time sitting, so do what you can to facilitate that. There is also a good bit of residual pain, so make sure she takes her pain medication on time. And if you can mind the baby while she naps, you will assist her recovery even more. Generally, within a week or 10 days, she will be feeling much more like her old self.

- For C-sections, other restrictions will apply. Her incision will restrict her movement, and she will be discouraged from doing stairs more than once or twice a day for a week or more. Pain management is a major priority, and she'll be restricted from driving for two weeks. Let her take her time to move, to stand up from a chair, or to walk up or down stairs. You'll help the most by assisting with the baby as much as you can as she recovers.

16. Momma Maintenance – Mood Swings

Your baby's mother is an emotional mess. The birth itself, the new requirements of motherhood, and the hormonal roller coaster of her post-pregnant state will make her moody, to say the least. This is normal. She will cry. She will cry standing still holding a baby blanket. She will cry when the baby won't nurse well.

She will cry when the baby does nurse well. And when she's not crying, she might be angry, immeasurably happy, or full of guilt or frustration over some little nothing. Again, this is normal. Try not to take it personally. She is not angry with you; she is tired and hormonal. She is not trying to be difficult; she is learning seventeen new things at once...and she's hormonal. Give her space. Help when you can. Listen. She will soon start to find a way back to an emotional evenness, but for now, just let her cry.

17. Momma Maintenance – Household Management

Now is a good time to chip in as much as you can. For now (and maybe for a few weeks or months), taking care of the baby is her highest priority. If she can get even one other chore done, that will be a good day. So look for ways to help out. Ask her, "Is there anything I can help you with right now?" Give her space to learn how to be a mom, but make yourself available, at least until things start to settle down.

18. Meet-the-Baby Mayhem (and How to Manage It)

People will want to visit after the baby is born. This is a good thing, especially if they volunteer to bring a meal, but it can also be a tiring and difficult time. Set some ground rules to make the introductions successful without being stressful. Here are a few examples:

- Require that everyone, even family, call before they come.
- Ask them to wash their hands before holding the baby (many will offer to do this – take them up on it!).
- Keep a close eye on your baby and the baby's mom. Are they still enjoying the visit? Is it getting tiring or stressful? Is it time for a feeding? What about your own dinner?

- It is okay for you to refuse a visit until later, let visitors know you need to get the baby fed, or otherwise control the visits. Be gracious and flexible, when possible, but do not hesitate to do whatever you can to make these meet-n-greets enjoyable for everyone, especially mom and baby.

19. Grandmothers

One of the hardest relationships to manage is with the newly minted grandmothers. Your baby's mom may want her mom there for help. You may prefer your mom to come. You may need both to come, at different times. Be flexible with your baby's mom and both of your mothers. They want to bond with their new grandchild, and unless there is good reason that cannot happen, you need to facilitate a good relationship on both sides. Whether that means splitting holidays or finding a different solution, talk with your baby's mom about what you both want and need so that you can, above all else, stay on the same page.

20. Daddy Time

The first hours and days after the birth of a baby are hard on everyone; even you. So what happens when you need a break? Take one. The more tired, stressed or overwhelmed you feel, the less you will be able to help and support your family. If you need a night out, do your best to get it. You may have to plan ahead. You may need to check with your baby's mom before making plans. You may need to work a little harder to get some time off, but do that work and enjoy some down time. You will be able to enjoy your new family more when you get it.

21. The New Rules of Boys' Time[11]

- Life is no longer easily scheduled. Even if you've always made last minute plans, don't assume that you can spring "Hey, Babe, I'll be late tonight" on a new mom without tears and frustration. Do your best to make plans in advance so that everyone can enjoy the down time.

- Non-dad friends may not get the new you. Your days are consumed with baby poop and sleep cycles, while they're still focused on ESPN. This is okay, but it may take some practice to find a good balance between your latest poop story and your friends' lives.

- You may find it easier now to hang with other couples or families. This is okay. Some old friends won't transition with you to this new adventure. Some new friends will come along. Try to be flexible. You will soon find good friendships again.

22. Returning to Work

Eventually, you will go back to work. When you do, you will need to find a new rhythm with your work-life balance. Here are some suggestions to help the transition go smoothly:

- Check in on your family through the day. Text or call to find out how things are going. Send your baby's mom flowers on your first day back to work. Do what you can to let her know that you are thinking of them, even though you aren't there.

- When you get home, ask how the day went. Don't be judgmental about the house, the laundry, the lack of dinner, or why she didn't get a shower. Offer to help in any way you can, even if it's holding the baby for a few minutes while she goes to the bathroom.

- Don't be too hard on yourself. You will make mistakes. You will be tired. You may not be able to take the 3 a.m. feeding and still be functional at work. Talk about these things with your baby's mom and work together to find a good solution for everyone.

Gear & Supplies

23. Prepping the Crib

- Avoid drop-side cribs.
- A "convertible crib" option is great - it can later become a toddler or twin-sized bed frame. But if you think more children may be in your future, consider buying a simple crib and get bigger beds as your children grow.
- Blankets or pillows are suffocation hazards, so avoid placing them in the crib.
- Do invest in waterproof pads and sheet protectors. Nighttime messes are much easier to address if you don't have to strip the baby's bed at 3 a.m.
- Bumpers are usually not recommended (the thick padding is a suffocation risk), but this is

not a great concern until your baby can move by herself. Also, you can buy mesh bumpers that protect your child from getting wrapped up in the crib slats without risking his breathing.
- Set your crib to the correct height (higher for newborns, lower as the child learns to pull up or stand). And don't throw away the instructions.

24. Nursery Necessities

- A crib or other sleeping arrangement for the baby.
- A dresser or closet to store clothes.
- A changing table with all the necessary supplies (see below)
- A chair for nursing and soothing. Rockers and gliders are nice, but an easy chair also has its advantages.
- All other additions to your nursery are helpful, generally acceptable, but not required.

25. Changing Table at the Ready

A well-stocked changing table should have the following:

- A changing pad with cover
- Diapers (start with NB or size 1)
- Wipes.
- Baby bottom supplies: diaper rash cream, petroleum jelly, etc.
- Easy access to changes of clothes or cloths to deal with blow-outs or accidents
- A nearby receptacle for used diapers.

26. Baby Stations Everywhere

Consider placing more than one changing "station" around the house. Each should be stocked with at least wipes and extra diapers and should be set up in the areas most commonly used for diaper changes: mom & dad's bedroom, the living room or family room, and the family vehicle (for on-the-go needs) are all good options.

27. Packing a Diaper Bag[12]

No matter what size or style you choose, a well-stocked diaper bag should include:

- Diapers & wipes
- A pacifier (if the baby takes one)
- Various liquid items: Diaper rash cream, hand sanitizer, lotion
- Changes of clothes (more than one)
- Bottles and formula (for non-breastfed babies)
- A nursing cover-up (for breastfed babies)
- A few easily transportable baby toys or books (easily cleanable is best)

Optional, but sometimes useful, items include:

- An extra shirt for baby's mom

- Travel-sized bottles of baby bath soap or shampoo
- Snacks or drink for mom
- Places for an adult's wallet, car keys, sunglasses and phone

28. Baby on the Move

A quick guide for putting your child in the car seat:

- Do not overdress the baby. Strap her into the car seat in regular clothes and cover her with a blanket to keep her warm. Heavy coats or coverings can keep the seat belt straps from working properly.
- Pull both shoulder straps to the sides of the car seat.
- Place the child into the seat and move her arms through each shoulder strap.

- Buckle the chest latch and snap both sides into the seat latch.

- Pull to tighten. Some straps pull from the child's feet. Others pull from the back or behind. Make sure you know how to tighten and loosen the straps quickly, and be sure that the straps are tight but not restrictive.

29. Cloth vs. Disposable: A Great Debate

- Disposable diapers are just what they sound like. These diapers are sold in bulk and contain various gels that absorb baby's "output" while keeping baby's bottom mostly dry. They can get expensive quickly, but they are convenient and easy.

- Cloth diapers are rectangles of cloth (pre-fold is usually preferred) that are folded and attached around the baby. Most cloth diapering options now use washable "outer" diapers with an inside

pocket to tuck in a cloth diaper or other liner. They then Velcro around the child like a disposable diaper.
- Both sides of this debate have pros and cons. Do your research and find the system that works for you.

30. Baby Goo and Other Essentials

- Baby wash: a combination shampoo and body wash that is designed to be gentle and avoid burning baby's eyes in the bath.
- Baby lotion: a creamy concoction, often with "soothing" scents, that you can rub on your baby after baths to avoid dry skin or to help relax her before bedtime.
- Diaper creams: white creams or clear ointments that create a moisture barrier to avoid or eliminate diaper rash. Watch for issues with sensitive skin, though. Some babies can react to

the diaper rash cream, adding to the redness instead of eliminating it.

- Cornstarch. An old-fashioned but still effective treatment for diaper rash. Spread it carefully to avoid creating a puff of powder into baby's face, but nothing works better for absorbing wetness.
- Petroleum jelly. A circumcised penis should be coated with petroleum jelly to keep the diaper from sticking until the wound heals completely.
- Baby soap and shampoo. You can buy separate soaps and shampoos for your baby. Differing brands can offer organic ingredients, extra lotion, or hypoallergenic options, so look for whatever will work best for your baby's hair and skin.

31. Sound Machines and Mobiles

- A mobile can be a helpful toy for entertaining baby in her crib. Some children learn to soothe themselves to a mobile that dangles above them or a crib toy that projects pictures onto the ceiling or plays music from the side of the crib. Other babies find these options distracting and will sleep less well when they are turned on. You will simply have to experiment with your baby's preferences.

- Sound machines are another sleep aid option. They play a variety of sounds from white noise to ocean tides to rain forest noises. Again, such sounds can help soothe the baby (like the shushing technique mentioned above), but some babies won't be greatly helped. Still, if your baby is not sleeping well, either of these options is worth a try.

32. It Goes Where?!? (Breast Pump Basics)

The breast pump is a helpful tool for every breastfeeding mom. Here's a basic run-down.

- Every pump consists of at least a breast shield, a valve and membrane, and a container for the milk. Hand-powered models require squeezing a handle repeatedly. Electric ones use a vacuum and tubes to pull the milk into the container.
- Electric pumps simulate how your baby actually gets milk from the breast. They stimulate the breast to start producing milk (called "let down") and then change the amount of "pull" so the milk is produced with greater speed and force.
- Breast pumps are not as effective as your baby at expressing milk, so it takes a few attempts before the breasts will let down milk in good quantities. But don't let your baby's mom get discouraged. Eventually, most women can get at

least 2-3 ounces of milk, per side, at each pumping session.

- If your baby's mother struggles with breastfeeding or pumping, there are usually lactation consultants available at the hospitals that are happy to help troubleshoot so that she can have a successful breastfeeding experience.

33. You'd Better Sit Down – Estimating Diaper Cost

The first year of disposable diapers can cost $500-$600. Using a cloth diaper service is similar in price though washing them at home is much cheaper. But washing them at home will also increase your water usage, your electric bill, and your detergent costs. So all in all, the two types of diapers will cost you approximately the same amount.[13]

Chapter Two: Month Two – What to Expect[14]

Your baby is now four weeks old. What a change, right? That little bundle of blankets you brought home from the hospital is now more alert and active. And while some of the original challenges are no longer an issue, brand new ones are popping up all the time. In this section, we will discuss your baby's development from week 4 to week 7, providing information to help you set expectations for your baby as well as for yourself.

Physically speaking, this month will be demanding for your little one. She will start to discover that her body came with arms and legs attached. While she's a long way from grabbing onto toys, she will spend hours staring at her hands in wonder. She will start to hold up her feet and move them around with (slightly) more intention and control. In this month, you will notice a significant change in her ability to hold her head erect. As her neck becomes stronger, she will be able to lift her own head and maintain her balance instead of just moving her head from side-to-side on your shoulder. Neck strength is also a good indicator that she is ready for more "tummy time." Let her spend a few minutes at a time on her stomach, either on the floor with you beside her or on your legs. This position forces her to use those neck muscles, developing her ability to control her head and look where she wants to look.

Your baby's senses are rapidly developing, too. She will start to develop new and varied facial expressions (some of them still cross-eyed). While she could barely focus her eyes when you brought her home from the hospital, she is able now to see clearly farther away from her. She'll love to have a mobile above her bed or pack-n-play. Toys with bright colors or black-and-white patterns will keep her interest now, and you can begin to introduce books and toys with pictures for her to look at and begin to learn.

Verbal skills are at an important stage in this month. You will be amazed at the sheer number (and volume) of sounds a baby can produce. She may start to "practice" sounds, discovering that she can squeal, coo, and even laugh. Interacting with her verbally will make a world of difference in her language development. "Talk" to her by repeating the sounds she makes. Using baby talk is totally fine because the pitch and sound actually draws your baby's attention to the sounds you are making. Have conversations with her, asking questions and leaving space for her to answer. This kind of interaction is the basis of her communication skills, her sense of how to talk and leave space for someone else to talk back.

Your baby may – or may not – be developing more effective eating and sleeping patterns now. At this stage, many babies begin to go longer between feedings, though every three hours is still normal. You and the baby's mom have probably found a workable routine by now, but if not, don't worry. Your circumstances can affect the development of a routine. A baby with colic or reflux will make nighttime rest very difficult. Other factors such as returning to work, the success of breastfeeding or other physical issues may keep you from a good routine. Give your family room to try different options until you find one that works. Every family is different, and you will eventually find the patterns that work best for you.

Now is also a good time to introduce new toys and new experiences to your baby. Experiment with different kinds of music. Offer new toys and textures. Rub different fabrics on her hands and feet. Take your little one out in the world with you – to the grocery, on a walk, to the park. While you need to pay close attention to signs of overstimulation (extreme fussiness, looking away, or arching her back may indicate that she needs a break), have fun introducing her to the all-new-to-her world in which we live.

Your baby will blossom in uncountable ways in this month. Her personality will start to reveal itself. You may discover some of your baby's ticklish spots or see her newborn hair fall out and be replaced by baby hair – of a totally different color! Her ability to express her needs (and your ability to understand her) will develop rapidly. You will start to discover that your baby is a real person with a will, personal preferences, and opinions about how the world will go. It is the start of a real relationship, and one that will only grow stronger as you continue into the next month and after.

Month Two: Tips & Tricks

<u>Baby Basics</u>

34. Baby Gas and Burping Techniques

- Babies get gas bubbles from swallowing air while they eat. These bubbles can be uncomfortable, resulting in a very fussy baby.
- Shoulder techniques. Put the baby up on your shoulder with her belly at your shoulder level. Alternate patting and rubbing the baby's back to see if you can move the offending bubble.
- Lap technique. Lay the baby on her stomach on your lap with her head supported on your knees. Gently pat and rub her back.
- Sometimes switching between the shoulder and the lap can help her burp. And don't forget the wonders of gas drops for a regularly gassy baby.

35. A Pooping Primer[15]

Most babies have normal, regular poop most of the time. However, at some point, you will encounter the poop extremes: diarrhea and constipation.

- Diarrhea is very runny, even watery, comes in a variety of colors, and will usually leak out of diapers. Diarrhea can quickly lead to dehydration in an infant, so call your doctor if the baby has multiple bouts of diarrhea in a day or for multiple days in a row.

- Constipation is an entirely different matter of concern. Breastfed babies actually poop less regularly (once a week is not uncommon), which is not the same issue. Constipation can look like hard, pebble-shaped poop, and it is usually not a long-term problem. However, some babies may need water, pear juice or prune juice to help "move things along."

36. Master of the Bath[16]

Once your newborn loses her umbilical cord, she is ready for a full-body bath.

- Using a sink or infant bathtub may work well for your infant. However, it is possible to use a full-size tub with just a couple of inches of warm (not hot) water.

- Be sure to support her head and neck while you are bathing her.

- Wash her face first, her head next, and then the rest of her body, ending with her diaper area. This prevents germs from being spread to her sensitive eyes.

- Wet babies are very slippery. Be very careful to keep a good hold on her. You may even put a washcloth on the bottom of the sink or tub to keep her bottom from sliding around.

- Babies do not need to be bathed daily unless it is to clean up a diaper mess. Most infants will do well with 2-3 baths per week.

- Some babies find baths very soothing. Feel free to play with her in the warm water, swishing it around her body and talking to her. Other infants will scream from the second the bath begins until you towel them dry. In this case, you will quickly learn to give speed baths!

37. Coping with the Crying[17]

Here are some new techniques you can try to help soothe your fussy baby:

- Most babies' cry because they're hungry, need a diaper change, or are tired. So start by offering a bottle (or breast), checking the diaper, and trying to settle your infant for a nap.

- Try slipping your (clean) pinkie into the baby's mouth. She may suck on it, helping to stop the crying and calm her down.

- Swaddle the baby or use a baby sling or carrier and walk around with her.

- Check for a temperature, try giving gas drops, or evaluate whether she doesn't feel well.

- Wait it out. Put the baby into the bouncy seat, swing, or lay her in her crib. The motion or vibration of the seat or the lack of stimulation may be just what she needs to calm down.

38. Will I Ever Sleep Through The Night Again?

Yes, but it probably won't be tonight.

39. Quick Change Artist

- Changing a baby's clothes can be complicated and difficult. Snaps, buttons and buckles are cute, but can be a pain to manage quickly (or at 3 a.m.). And be sure to support the baby's head when putting on or taking off her clothes.

- Try kimono or side-snap onesies for under pajamas. These do not snap between the baby's legs so they make nighttime diaper changes much faster.

- Diaper blowouts can be difficult to manage when the baby is dressed. Try running a little bath water and putting the baby into it fully clothed. Then you can pull off the clothes, quickly bathe the baby, and soak the poopy clothes in one easy step.

40. Colic

Colic is a condition of intense and lengthy bouts of crying. More than just fussiness, colic is defined as crying for three or more hours, three or more days a week, for three or more weeks in a row. A colicky baby is inconsolable and will cry all day or all night. Colic often peaks around 6 weeks, but may not resolve completely until the baby is 3-4 months old. If this describes your baby, talk to your pediatrician.[18]

41. The Lowdown on Reflux

Some babies struggle with acid reflux, often caused by an immature valve in the esophagus.[19] It can show up as a range of problems from discomfort to projectile vomiting. If your baby screams when you lay her down, especially flat on her back at bedtime, check with your doctor about reflux.

42. When to Call the Doctor[20]

For a baby under 3 months old, you should always call the doctor for a fever of 100.4 degrees or higher. For other concerns, such as a sudden change in appetite, a change in poop type or color, an unusual amount of inconsolable crying, or just a sense that your baby isn't acting like herself, you can often contact the on-call or triage nurse at your doctor's office for advice on what you should do.

43. Baby's 2-Month Checkup

Your infant's next well-visit will look very much like her previous ones. Her growth chart will be updated, and the doctor will examine her. Do bring questions that you have about her behavior or changes or about what you should expect in the near future.

44. Vaccinations

One of the major debates for parents is whether or not to vaccinate their children. First vaccinations will happen at these early well visits, so you will want to do your research early. Most doctors recommend vaccinations on schedule, but may be willing to modify the schedule of shots if you ask. Some pediatricians will not see a family that chooses not to vaccinate at all, so make sure you ask about that policy when you are deciding which doctor to choose.

45. Binky or Thumb?

Babies suck on things to soothe themselves. Some children are thumb-suckers from the day they are born. Others happily take to a pacifier. Some prefer to soothe themselves with a blankie or lovey, and all of these options are fine. While there is some concern that long-term thumb sucking can affect tooth development or speech patterns, at this early stage, it is fine to let your baby pop her digit into her mouth. And it's fine to introduce a pacifier at this age as well. Whatever works to soothe and calm your baby is a great benefit, especially if it results in another hour or two of sleep!

46. Nail Care 101[21]

You will, at some point, need to trim your baby's finger and toenails. Here's a quick guide to the process.

- You need to trim your baby's nails weekly. They grow fast and keeping them short will prevent her from scratching herself and you.

- Choose either a pair of nail clippers or nail scissors for the process.

- Trim carefully around the curve of each nail. You may get too close at times, especially if the baby pulls her hand or foot away. Just do the best you can.

- Many people recommend trimming nails right after bath, while the baby is asleep or while the baby is distracted (such as with a feeding). Find what time is best for you.

You, Her & Them

47. Momma Maintenance – "The Checkup"

At six to eight weeks postpartum, your baby's mom will see her OB-GYN for a postpartum checkup. They will do a physical exam to make sure everything is healing well. They will chat about her adjustment, going back to work, and whether or not it's okay to return to more normal activities, such as exercise and sex. You will also want to chat about post-baby birth control before this appointment, as now is the time the doctor will prescribe whatever option you decide is best for the your family.

48. Momma Maintenance – Love Life...or Lack Thereof

Of course, these last six to eight weeks may have been a long wait for you. You may be excited to return to the bedroom with your baby's momma, but just keep in mind that a doctor's permission alone may not make that transition an easy one. Sex may be painful at first for her. She may be so exhausted that she struggles to be excited for sex. She may be concerned about her new body and whether she will be attractive. Communication is the key in this area. Tell her what you need. Assure her of your interest, but do not push. She will likely become more interested as the days go by, but try to give her the space she needs to rejoin you in the bedroom with excitement.

49. Momma Maintenance – PPD[22]

Adjusting emotionally is one of the most difficult shifts a woman makes post-pregnancy. You need to be alert for signs of PPD, postpartum depression, which can surface immediately or even months after the baby is born. Some of the warning signs for this difficult condition are insomnia; crying that persists all day, lack of interest in activities or people, change in appetite, excessive guilt, and anxiety. There are other symptoms, but if your baby's mom is showing these symptoms, encourage her to talk to her doctor and get help.

50. Momma Maintenance – Household Management

Now is a good time to chat about how your household is running. Do you need to pick up another chore or two? Is your baby's momma feeling more on top of keeping the house or is the baby still taking up the vast majority of her time? What can you do, together, to keep your house and family working well? Spend some time talking about these kinds of issues.

51. Momma Maintenance – Back to Work or Stay at Home?

By now, your baby's mom may be gearing up to return to work. Some moms take maternity leave, thinking they'll happily return in six weeks, only to find they love being home. Other moms are ready to go back to life outside, even though they will miss their baby. Be open to her concerns and issues. Does she want to go back? Does she *have* to go back, whether she wants to or not? Is she feeling stressed? Guilty? Excited? Find time to chat about these topics, and be as open as you can with each other. It will make her decision, whatever it is, easier to manage.

52. Daddy's Deal – Finding a Groove[23]

Some dads fall into fatherhood with joy and enthusiasm. They read the books, take the classes, and change the diapers. Other dads are more laid back, even reticent to get involved. Are you struggling with resentment for all the changes that have happened? Are you finally getting a groove again? It's okay not to love every part of parenting (no one does). It's okay to want some time to yourself or to occasionally wish for your easy-going life back. This is normal. Talk about it with your baby's mom and don't forget to enjoy the little one who fills so much of your day.

53. Daddy's Deal – Dads and Depression[24]

Depression isn't just for new moms anymore. Some new dads, stay-at-home or not, struggle with depression after the baby is born. If you find yourself withdrawing from your family or home life or if you're struggling with anxiety or insomnia, get some help. Talk to a doctor or counselor. Don't try to soldier on alone. Get help.

54. Holiday Hoopla

Holiday season may be quickly approaching or it may yet be months away, but sooner or later, your new family is going to have to join a holiday gathering. You should start talking to each other about what you want that visit to look like. Think about what changes your new baby will make for your normal travel plans and try to consider what you should take and what you can do without. Your first major family gathering can be stressful, but planning ahead can make a lot of difference.

55. Hanging with the Guys

If you haven't made time to hang with some of your guy friends, now is a good time. While your baby may not be sleeping steadily through the night, you probably have a decent routine down. Again, it would be wise to check with baby's mom, but start looking for opportunities to meet up with your friends and recharge.

Gear & Supplies

56. Getting Baby Out of the House – A How-To

- At Home
    - Gather the things you will need: diaper bag, car seat, etc.
    - Check the diaper bag to ensure you have all the supplies you might need while you're out.

- Look at the clock. When is baby's next feeding? Do you have time to run your errand and get back before then? Add 20 minutes. Babies can make any outing more complicated or time-consuming. Do you still have enough time?
- Pack the baby in the car seat and move everything to the car. Do a quick check for anything you forgot. Drive away.

- At Stores/Businesses
  - Park near a cart return. It's easier to snap the car seat in place, transfer your bags, and push the cart in than it is to walk the cart to a faraway return after you've stowed your purchases.
  - At some point, you will be the dad of "that" kid, the one screaming in Aisle 12 while people look askance at you. It's okay. Babies

cry. But it might be good to curtail your shopping trip quickly (or find the nearest family restroom and change that diaper).

- Be prepared for people to stop to see your baby. They will compliment you. They will ask inappropriate questions. They will give you unsolicited advice. Feel free to ignore them. Feel free to thank them kindly and walk away. Babies just have that effect on people.

57. Burp Cloths and Everything Waterproof

By this time your baby will be filling diapers like a champ. Sometimes until they overflow. For this issue, and all the other ways that babies can cover you, her mom, and the furniture, floor and walls with wetness, you will need protection.

- Burp cloths are not technically waterproof, but they are handy go-to spill cleaners. You can also use cotton receiving blankets for a variety of uses, other than swaddling. For a child with severe reflux, for example, receiving blankets are the only big-enough burp cloth.

- Waterproof bedding options abound. Invest in multiple waterproof crib pads in varying sizes and styles. You can even buy waterproof fabric from a fabric store, cut it to fit your crib, and use that as well.

- You will need a variety of sheet changing pad protectors. Terry fabric on one side and waterproofed on the other, these go on top of sheets or changing pad covers to absorb an initial mess with a still-clean cover underneath. Very handy.

58. Baby Wearing Bingo

Another big point of discussion is baby wearing. This phrase refers to using a sling or other carrier to literally wear your baby wherever you go. There are pros and cons to the approach; some parents are very much for it, and others are very opposed. Just think of it this way: A sling or carrier can be a very useful piece of equipment for any parents to have available. The amount of time you put your child in a carrier is entirely up to you and the baby's mother.

59. Cold as Ice: A Breast Milk Storage Primer[25]

- Store breast milk only in approved bags or bottles. Always write on the package the date the milk was expressed.

- Store breast milk in small amounts (1-3 ounces) to make defrosting easier. It also allows you to make exactly the amount of milk the baby needs without wasting any.

- Storage options:
  - Breast milk is good at room temperature for 4-6 hours.
  - Store it in a cooler with ice pack for up to 24 hours.
  - Refrigerate breast milk for 3-8 days or freeze it for 6-12 months, depending on your freezer type.

60. Ten Things Every 2-month old DOESN'T Need[26]

- A wipes warmer
- Actual shoes.
- A crib **and** a bassinet
- A high chair
- Educational videos
- Diaper stacker (for the nursery)

- Bath thermometer
- Special detergent
- Pacifier wipes
- Stuffed animals

61. IMS: Infant Medical Supplies

Here are a few items that you will need in your medical toolkit, even for your infant.

- Baby medicines. It is unlikely that you will need medicines for your baby in the first three months, but it doesn't hurt to have them on hand. If necessary, acetaminophen can be used for infants, but ibuprofen is not safe for babies under 6 months of age.

- Saline drops or spray/bulb syringe. While it is unlikely your newborn will catch a cold at this stage, it is possible she will catch one by the time she is three months old. Saline drops loosen the mucous in her nose, making it easier to remove with the bulb syringe. She will hate having her nose suctioned this way, but it is better than listening to her stuffiness as she tries to sleep and eat.

- Gas drops. These are liquid gold for a gassy baby. Keep them on hand especially for when you cannot seem to move a gas bubble with the other techniques.

- Thermometer: There are lots of options and all of them work well. Just make sure you know how to use and read yours correctly before taking your baby's temperature.

62. Swagger Wagon: A Stroller Primer

- You will, at some point, need a stroller for transporting your little one. Some families use a travel system, a matching set of stroller, car seat and car seat base. You can also purchase each of these items separately, though you need to make sure that all of the items will work together.

- Install a car seat base in every car your baby will ride in. It makes switching cars much easier if all you have to do is unlatch the car seat and snap it into the base in the second vehicle.

- You can also invest in a stroller frame: a metal frame on wheels that accommodates a variety of car seat types and brands. It is usually more lightweight than the travel system strollers, so it fits well in smaller vehicles.

63. Entertainment Extravaganza

There are a variety of stationary entertainers for infants. You may not need them all, but having one or two available could be useful.

- Baby swing. These come in all sorts of designs and colors, with all sorts of sounds and moving parts. They can be full-sized, travel-sized, even a frame to turn your car seat into a swing. You don't need a thousand bells and whistles: just a swinging seat and music will do.

- Bouncers or Bouncy seats. They also come in many styles and colors. They often have a vibrating option so the baby can be buzzed to sleep (and it works!), and a toy bar that snaps into the frame so the baby can see the dangling characters. These can be expensive or inexpensive, but they can often be a lifesaver for the parents of a fussy or reflux-prone baby.

- Exersaucer or Activity Seat. Your infant is much too young for this level of entertainer, but it's good to have one in mind (or in the box) for future use. Most babies won't be ready for this type of seat until they are about 6 months old.

64. Ten Things Every 2-month old DOES Need

- A place to sleep.

- Clothes to wear.

- Food to eat.

- Diapers.

- Swaddling blankets.

- Snuggling.

- Interaction with Mom and Dad.

- Car seat.

- Diaper bag

- A clean, loving home.

65. Music

Music can be one of the most effective ways to soothe and quiet an infant. Even at these early weeks, babies can be influenced by music. Soothing, quiet lullabies can be a great way to help your baby fall asleep. Singing to her, even silly songs that you make up, teach her about rhythm, about language, and about social connections. Have fun with the music that you play for your baby, and don't limit yourself to only "kids" music. It is possible to find good, not-annoying music designed for kids, but feel free to introduce her to music of all types and cultures from the very beginning.

66. Kids Clothes – Needs, Wants, and that Kid in the Baby Gap Ad

No matter what "they" say, no matter how "cute" the clothes, no baby *needs* outfits that cost more than a pair of your jeans. When purchasing clothes, buy things that you like and that fit your family's style. But keep in mind that these clothes will be spit up on, pooped on, and otherwise stained. All your child really needs is some good, basic clothes: onesies, sleepers (for sleep and for awake time), one-piece outfits, socks or booties, and a few dressier outfits for photos, church, or family gatherings.[27]

Chapter 3: Month Three – What to Expect[28]

Your little one is now almost three months old. She has crossed out of the newborn stage and into the infant stage. She is learning new things every day and presenting new challenges as well. At this stage you will begin to see your baby leave behind some behaviors and offer you instead tiny hints of things to come.

At three months, your baby will probably weigh 12-15 lbs. and will now be 23-24 inches long. Most babies follow an accepted schedule for well-visits, seeing a pediatrician or doctor at one week, one month, two months, four months, six months, nine months and one year. At each of these visits, measurements of the baby's height, weight, and head circumference are recorded so that her growth can be compared to other children the same age. Some parents' put a lot of focus on this growth chart, fretting about what percentile their child is, but these charts are not gold standards. Every child is different and develops at their own pace, so the real goal is to see children grow gradually and steadily at each well visit.[29]

In Month Two, your baby began to strengthen muscles and gain control especially of her head and neck. In this month, she will continue to improve in these areas. She will gain stability in her upper body so that she can begin to push herself up when she's on her tummy in a sort of mini-pushup move. This is the beginning of her ability to roll herself from front-to-back, so give her lots of opportunity to practice. She will also start becoming more coordinated overall. Instead of flailing her arms and legs, she will begin to move them intentionally and with control, bringing her fingers to her mouth over and over just to practice her aim. She may begin to reach for toys, knocking them with her hands, and she may be able to grasp a toy you place in her hand, though she will not be able to grab one by herself for a few more weeks.

You may discover other new physical realities show up at this time. Some babies drool heavily, and you may need to make bibs a coordinating part of your baby's wardrobe. Some parents find they need to change bibs throughout the day, and if that is the case, you will need to watch for a rash that can develop in the constantly moist area around the neck and chin. As your child begins to eat more at each feeding, or if your child struggles with reflux, her ability to projectile vomit may also increase at this time. It's nothing to worry about – she still will get plenty of nutrition from what wasn't projected across your lap – but you will probably need to find larger burp cloths.

In Month Three, your baby will also develop longer patterns in her eating and sleeping cycle. Much to the relief of anyone taking a night shift, the baby may start to go 4 hours between feedings at night, though you cannot expect the average baby to sleep longer until they are at least 13 pounds. So far, you may have simply let the baby sleep wherever the baby likes to sleep (bouncy seats or swings, for example), but this is an excellent time to begin putting her down in her crib and encouraging her to sleep there. It is still important to lay her down on her back and keep the crib clear of blankets and other suffocation hazards. But with a little trial and error, it is usually not long before the child can be trusted to nap happily in her room instead of in her swing.

Emotionally and socially, your child will truly start to shine. She will recognize your face and voice. You will be rewarded with small smiles, gurgles, and coos that actually signal her pleasure at seeing you, instead of merely gas bubbles. She will begin to develop relationships with others, as well: siblings, grandparents, and familiar caregivers. As they talk and smile at her, she will learn to smile and respond to them, effectively preparing her for future social interactions. Do keep in mind, however, that your baby's personality will become more obvious here. A naturally shy baby may not enjoy a stranger's attention while an outgoing infant will welcome all interactions. Start paying attention to your baby's cues and help her, whenever possible, to manage social connections positively.

Month Three: Tips & Tricks

<u>Baby Basics</u>

67. Keep Out Da Stink: Diaper Keeping Strategies

There are generally two main diaper keepers: the Diaper Champ and the Diaper Genie. Both use a special lid to keep odors inside. The primary difference is that the "Champ" uses regular kitchen-sized garbage bags, and the "Genie" requires specially packaged bags. Both let out a little smell when they are opened to change bags. Another option is to throw the used diapers away in a regular garbage can (either in the kitchen or garage) and keep them out of the nursery altogether.

68. Baby Movement Guide

Babies in Month Three are not even close to mobility. But their movements are preparing the way for that first roll, first crawl, and first step. Right now, you will watch your infant open and close her hand, over and over, learning to control the movement. She will kick her legs while she's on her back, trying to manage not just her legs, but the rest of her body, too. She is learning balance. She is perfecting her head and neck control. All of these will eventually be required for those first real movements. So give your baby time and encourage all of those movements as much as you can.

69. Play with Me![30]

Play helps the baby learn about her body and her world, and it encourages bonding as well. Here are some quick tips for playing with your baby right now:

- Don't be afraid to move her. Just do it gently. Babies can be "danced" or rocked on your lap. Lay her down and move her hands and feet while singing "Patty-Cake" or "If You're Happy and You Know It." Pull her up by the arms so that she practices holding her own head (lay her down quickly). Stand her up on her feet (with you completely supporting her) so she can practice bearing weight on her legs.

- Stare at her. Make silly faces. Hold her so she can look around and tell her about all the things nearby.

- Read to her. Get "first" books that have textures and big pictures. Help her touch all the fabrics and describe what is there. And when that gets boring (and it will), go ahead and read the sports page or business section to her, too.

70. Tips for an Effective Bedtime Routine[31]

- There is no right way to do bedtime.

- Try a variety of activities: singing, reading books, baths, snuggling, rocking.

- Don't try to force a routine. Watch your baby's rhythms and try to work with them.

- Don't stress if it doesn't happen every night. Missing a night or even two will not cause any major problems. Do a routine as often as you can, and don't worry.

"Do You Want to be My Love-y?"

A lovey is a toy or object that a baby attaches to. Some babies choose a lovey almost immediately: a blanket or toy that she finds comforting. Other babies will not attach to a lovey for a year or more. There is nothing wrong with either side of this spectrum. If your baby loves the feel of a particular blanket while she falls asleep, keep it handy. If she has no real interest in any toys or objects- no worries. Just make sure the object of her attachment never poses a suffocation risk.

71. Getting Some Sleep

- There is no such thing as a "normal" sleep pattern for any baby until they are at least 12 weeks old.[32]

- Don't compare your baby to other babies, especially in the area of sleep. Focus on *your* baby's sleep, comparing this week's pattern to last week's or the week before.

- Find a sleep arrangement that works for your family. Some families choose to co-sleep, keeping the baby near mom (either in the same bed or in a crib in the same room). Other families use a nursery with a baby monitor. There is no right way. The goal is to meet everyone's needs and still get sleep.

72. Personality Peeks

You should be getting some good hints about the little person that you brought home from the hospital a few short weeks ago. Have you noticed that she likes to be with people or cries when she's alone in her room? Does she like baths or hate them? Is she a determined eater or very laid back? While her full personality won't show up all at once, you can start to pay attention to what she is showing you now. All of these things are signals about what you can expect in the very near future.

73. Tummy Time Tips[33]

Tummy Time is very important. Lay her down on her tummy and encourage her to look up at you and to lift her head and chest off the blanket. Keep her from burying her face, but give her time to try out her muscles, too. Prop her on a pillow if she can't hold herself up for very long. Tummy time does not have to long to be effective. A few minutes every day will make a huge difference.

74. Breast or Bottle, Revisited

When a new baby arrives, most parents are already committed to a feeding style. We are *going* to breastfeed. I am *definitely* using formula. However, now that you and your little one have been eating together for a number of weeks, how is your initial choice going? Revisit the topic with your baby's mom. Is she really enjoying nursing, or is it just adding stress to her life? Is the baby getting good at eating, or is every feeding time a nightmare? Have illness or a return to work changed things? Talk to your baby's momma and help her evaluate where things are and whether or not you need to try a different option. It is okay to change course, and now is a good time to make any needed changes.

75. Find a Good Pediatrician[34]

Not every pediatrician is great for every family. Concerns about bedside manner, philosophical differences, and office policies may have left you feeling ignored, misunderstood, or even irritated with your baby's doctor. Do not feel obligated to remain at a given practice simply because you started there. Your family needs a doctor that you can trust and who gives you the help you really need. Some qualities of a good pediatrician include:

- An open, empathetic demeanor
- Extensive knowledge of babies and their needs
- Intentional commitment to listen to you and answer your questions
- A good reputation

- Clear and effective office policies

If your doctor does not have these basic qualities, it may be best for your baby and your family to find a different, more suitable office.

76. Infant Illnesses

Infants who get even a few weeks of breast milk are usually protected from serious infections or colds because they get their mother's immunity through the milk. However, even breastfed babies can get sick. Here is a very basic list of things you might see.

- Rashes, red bumps or circles on the skin are common in even small babies. Most are harmless, such as a heat rash or redness under a drooler's chin. But they can get infected if they go undetected. So be sure to check them regularly and keep the baby's skin as dry as possible in those areas.

- Some rashes are caused by a virus and can appear after the virus has already run its course. But these rashes, such as Roseola, always follow a high fever. And a fever over 100.4 degrees in a baby under 3 months old should **always** be checked by a doctor. [35]

- Thrush is a fungal infection that creates white patches in and around the baby's mouth. It will go away on its own, but if you see these white spots or patches, call your doctor. There is medicine that can be given to make sure it clears up quickly.[36]

- Skin issues such as cradle cap or eczema are common in infants. These conditions often look like dry patches or scales on the scalp (cradle cap) or the rest of the body (eczema). Your doctor will help you treat these conditions, which are not serious, even if they are persistent.[37]

- Changes in "normal" behavior are a major concern with infants this young. A normally calm baby who screams non-stop for hours or an active baby who suddenly seems listless should make you start paying attention for other signs that something may be wrong. Call your doctor immediately if you suspect your child is ill. And always trust your parental instinct. If you just have a sense that something is wrong...check into it.

77. Starting Solids or Too Soon?

In Month Three, your baby should not be eating anything but breast milk or formula. Even cereal is not appropriate for a child this age.

78. Stubborn Baby, Stressed Parents

At this point, it is okay to follow your baby's lead in a number of areas. She will not be spoiled, and she is not willfully trying to make your life difficult. No matter what you believed before about thumb-sucking or loveys or breastfeeding or any other baby matter, your actual child has arrived with real natural leanings and her own personality. If she is a thumb-sucker and refuses every pacifier she is offered, try to accept that and fight the battle when she's older. If baby's mom always dreamed of breastfeeding, but the child cannot or will not latch, do your best to help her adjust to the idea that formula may be necessary. There is plenty you can do to help your child develop well. Don't focus on the negatives and lose sight of the lovely child you have.

You, Her & Them

79. Exhaustion. It's Exhausting.

Hopefully, by now, you are getting more sleep. But even if nighttime feedings are now 3-4 hours apart, you may still be waking up multiple times a night. This is the hardest stage, where the newness has worn off and the exhaustion has set in. This is normal. Now is the time that you must put in place good communication habits (talk to your baby's momma instead of arguing with her) and helpful ways to get extra rest. Go to bed on time. Take some time to relax. Make getting as much sleep as you can a priority. It will help you survive until that glorious moment when your baby sleeps through the night for the very first time.

80. Tips for Getting (Useful) Help.

People, even complete strangers, are always happy to hand out unsolicited advice about your child and your parenting skills. And while that kind of assistance isn't really helpful, sometimes you do need an extra hand. To get the help your family may need:

- Ask for help. From parents or family members who can babysit to friends who might be willing to bring a meal, no one will know you need something until you ask for it.

- Talk it out. Does your baby's mom need more help from you? Do you need a break from a certain chore that you hate? She cannot read your mind any more than you can read hers, so say it (kindly) out loud.

- Lower your expectations. If you cannot afford to hire a housekeeping service, then you might have to let go of some of the little chores that just aren't going to get done right now. And this is okay. Not every chore is the highest priority. Focus on your family first, then the most important chores, and do what you can for the other issues, as you are able.

81. Momma Maintenance – Hormone Checkup

Go back to Month Two and review the signs for postpartum depression. Talk through them with your baby's momma and make sure that she is not struggling with this disease. If she is, make sure she talks to her doctor and gets the help she needs.

82. Momma Maintenance – Bad Mom Syndrome

Moms feel judged by other moms. Even if no one is actually condemning your family's practices or mom's particular choices, just looking on Pinterest or Facebook can bring negative feelings. Remind your baby's momma that she is a good mom, the best one for your baby. Remind her that someone else's skills or strengths (have you seen how some people decorate the nursery?) are not indictments of her skills and strengths. Help her focus on all the good things she is doing because she will feel, on some days, that she isn't doing a single thing right.

83. Momma Maintenance – The Really Bad Day

At some point in these first three months, your baby's mom will have The Really Bad Day. This will be the day you come home to find her sobbing in her pajamas surrounded by a messy house or the day she comes home from work and sobs because she can't handle everything on her plate. This is normal. She is not a bad mom. She had a bad day. Help her evaluate what her goals are and, perhaps, help her to set more realistic goals for what she can reasonably accomplish taking care of a home and infant. Doing less is not a problem. Trying to do everything is.

84. Momma Maintenance – Back to Work and Surviving

Many mothers must return to work. Some get six weeks, some get twelve weeks, but for those moms who do go back to work, the transition will be difficult. She will cry. She will feel guilty for leaving her baby. She will wonder whether she's doing the right thing. Let her cry. Listen to her concerns. You should work together to find the best possible plan to manage your child and your household. She will make it over the hump, and she may be a better mom because she works. So support her and help her make the transition as smoothly as possible.

85. Daddy Time – Fitting It All In

Just like your baby's mom needs to have realistic expectations for herself, you need to evaluate your goals and expectations. You cannot do it all. You cannot be everything that everyone needs all the time. Talk through your roles and goals as a team. Make sure that your expectations for yourself (and her expectations for you) are reasonable and doable, so that you can support your family effectively.

86. Communication Keys[38]

- Talk regularly. Don't let issues or emotions build up. Set aside time every day, if possible, to talk together.

- Tone matters. Even if you are angry, use neutral words. Don't raise your voice, if possible. Let your tone stay calm.

- Choose your words carefully. Whether you are talking or responding to something she said, think before you speak.

- Be honest. Always.

- Remember that your little one will learn her communication patterns from you. Display the kind of dialogue that you want your baby to learn.

87. Setting Healthy Boundaries

Every family needs boundaries, between family members, between your family and your extended families, between your neighbors, friends, community and workplace.

- Good boundaries protect your family's priorities. Know what your family values and set your boundaries to defend those values.

- Good boundaries are flexible. There are exceptions to every rule. They should not be made often, but an occasional 'bending of the rules' is okay.

- Good boundaries are done as a team. These cannot be just *your* rules for your family. Talk with your baby's mom so you are on the same page as you communicate your boundaries to others.

- Extended family boundaries are necessary, but difficult to maintain. Do the best you can to make your mothers and family members happy, but always make sure your family is taken care of, even if is not what your family members want you to do.

88. Finding Good Connections – as a Family

As a family, try to start developing connections with other families. Use the groups you are already a part of – your church, your neighborhood, and your other social networks – as a starting point. You can also connect with people through local parenting groups, the library, and your child's day care center or through work. Just be open to getting together and making new friends with other families who can walk with you through the child-rearing years.

Gear & Supplies

89. Is this the Right Car Seat?

Even though your child is still an infant, you can choose between an infant car seat and a convertible seat. An infant seat is separate from its base so that you can pull the seat out without removing the baby first. A convertible seat is attached to the base and requires you to remove the baby every time. Both are designed to work with children as small as 7-10 pounds, but the infant seat only works until a child weighs 22-35 pounds[39] (at which point a convertible seat must be purchased), and a convertible seat works until the child weighs 65-80 lbs. Both have pros and cons, but a little research will help you decide which direction is right for your family.[40]

90. Top Ten Toys[41]

- Chunky board books
- Rattles
- Musical toys
- Mobiles
- Dangling toys (bouncy seat or play mat)
- Soft blocks & balls
- Teether toys
- Mirrors

- Bath toys
- Nesting/stacking toys

91. Controlling the Clutter

- Make use of bins and baskets
- Put everything where it goes every time it comes out
- Don't buy more than you need
- Buy as you need it (i.e., wait to purchase a high chair until baby is ready to use it)
- Use hidden spaces for storage (under the crib, for example)
- Be okay with some clutter; just don't let it run the house!

92. Baby-proof Now

- Do some baby-proofing before your child is mobile: cover electrical outlets, move breakable decorations to higher shelves, put away what you can't bear to lose, get window pulls and strings out of reach

- Other things – door knob covers, toilet locks, and coverings for corners or sharp edges – can be left undone until the child is actually moving.

- Some latches or locks you may never need. Just be sure that your home is a safe one for your little one.

93. Taking Great Pictures

- Get up close to your baby.

- Make sure your photos are well lit.

- Take as many pictures as you want, but don't be afraid to delete the "bad" ones (blurry ones, for example).

- Get pictures of the baby doing normal baby things; not every picture should be "staged."

- Do try to get pictures when the baby is fed and rested. A screaming baby will not be an easy one to capture well.

94. Thinking Ahead: Feeding Options

Between 4-6 months, you will introduce your child to real foods. Most families start with rice cereal or baby oatmeal because it's easy for the child to eat and because she is just learning to eat from a spoon. You will need some bowls and baby spoons, as well as the food itself. A high chair will be useful at that point as well.

95. Thinking Ahead: High Chairs

High chairs come in a number of styles. Space-saving high chairs strap to a regular adult chair so the baby sits at the table from the beginning. Foldable options can be folded up and put away when not in use, which works well for small spaces. Stand-alone high chairs are also available and come with a detachable tray on which the baby eats. Some of these chairs can also be all-in-one chairs, changing into space-saving or toddler seats as needed. Regardless of style, most seats have a variety of options such as reclining backs, washable covers or seats, and 5-point harnesses for safety.

96. Thinking Ahead: Baby Gates

One day, weeks from now, your baby will begin to move. And once she starts, she will just keep going. You may want to invest in some baby gates to help contain and direct her movements or keep her from stairs and off-limits rooms. Baby gates can be wood or plastic. They can be attached to the wall, or they can be held in place by tension (think curtain rods). If you have pets, you may already be using these gates to keep pets and babies apart, but it is good to think about where you will need gates before your baby crawls.

97. Baby Carriers

Babies are portable. While many parents use the infant car seat as the baby's primary mode of transportation, there are some times when a smaller option may work. In this case, consider a baby carrier. These are stationary seats that are strapped onto an adult's body. Sometimes the carrier is an actual frame. Other styles use fabric, wrapped around the body, to create a seat and hold the baby in place. You can also find slings or carriers with full metal frames (for hiking), so the options are nearly endless. Research the styles you think will work best for you, but if possible, try that style out before you buy. Borrow them from friends or see if the store will let you examine the carrier to help you decide which one will really be the right one for you.

98. Great Apps for Families[42]

You probably used a number of apps and online trackers before your baby was born. But now that she has arrived, there are lots of apps that you can use to help your family connect and stay organized.

- Cozi family organizer – this app offers a full array of family organizers, including a calendar, a shareable to-do list, and other helpful ways to keep all your information accessible and available.

- My Baby Today – an app by BabyCenter that gives helpful information about your baby and her development on the go.

- Instagram – a good example of a photo app that you may already be using. Make sure you can take and organize your pictures with this or a similar app.

- Other options – you can find apps for everything from finding rest stops on a trip to dictation apps that let you record your to-do list when you don't have a hand free to write it down. Ask other parents what apps they use and love and make good use of these tools for your family.

99. Relax

You've made it through more than two months already with your child. Your newborn is now a large part of your life and you can rest assured that your baby will grow up loving you for all the effort you have put in to nurturing her.

Conclusion

Your baby's first three months are tiring, difficult and amazingly rewarding. During these few weeks you are getting to know a new little person that you helped to create. The information presented here will help you manage and move forward, but it is just the tip of the iceberg. There is so much more to discover. As you and your little one move forward, you can build on these tips to create a home and family that will bring much joy for years to come.

Final Word/About the Author

I was born and raised in Norwalk, Connecticut. Growing up, I could often be found spending afternoons reading in the local public library about management techniques and leadership styles, along with overall outlooks towards life. It was from spending those afternoons reading about how others have led productive lives that I was inspired to start studying morning meditation. Usually I write works around sports to learn more about influential athletes in the hopes that from my writing, you the reader can walk away inspired to put in an equal if not greater amount of hard work and perseverance to pursue your goals. If there were one key takeaway from this book it would be that when it comes to raising a child, it ultimately comes down to experience and learning quickly. There are tons of things you must learn as a new dad and so you must adopt a positive outlook on learning everything you can so that you can best provide for your child If you enjoyed *Becoming a Father: What New Dads Should Expect & 99 Baby Tips to Survive Your Newborn's First Three Months*, please leave a review! Also, if you're a sports junkie, you can read more of my works on *Gratitude, How to Fundraise, How to Get Out of the Friend Zone, Histrionic Personality Disorder, Narcissistic Personality Disorder, Avoidant Personality Disorder, Sundown Syndrome, ISTJs, ISFJs, ISFPs, INTJs, INFPs, INFJs, ESFPs, ESFJs, ESTJs, ENFPs, ENFJs, ENTJs, How to be Witty, How to be Likeable, How to be Creative, Bargain Shopping, Productivity Hacks, Morning Meditation, 33 Life Lessons: Success Principles, Career Advice & Habits of Successful People* in the Kindle Store.

Like what you read?

I write because I love sharing personal development information on topics like how to raise children with fantastic readers like you. My readers inspire me to write more so please do not hesitate to let me know what you thought by leaving a review! If you love books on life, basketball, or productivity, check out my website at claytongeoffreys.com to join my exclusive list where I let you know about my latest books. Aside from being the first to hear about my latest releases, you can also download a free copy of *33 Life Lessons: Success Principles, Career Advice & Habits of Successful People*. See you there!

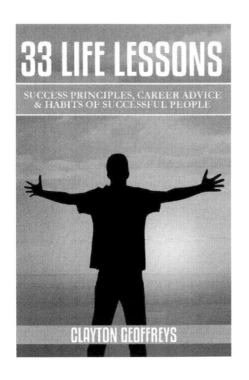

Endnotes

1. "Baby Development, Month by Month." BabyCenter.com. http://www.babycenter.com/303_baby-development-month-by-month_10380179.bc

2. Denise Schipani. "10 Newborn Worries (Not to Fret About)." Parents.com. http://www.parents.com/baby/care/newborn/newborn-worries-not-to-worry-about1/

3. Evonne Lack. "5 Things You Didn't Know About Newborns." BabyCenter.com. http://www.babycenter.com/0_5-things-you-didnt-know-about-newborns_10357995.bc

4. Emily Bloch. "Baby Poop: A Complete Guide." BabyCenter.com.

    http://www.babycenter.com/0_baby-poop-a-complete-guide_10319333.bc

5. "Guide to Firsts: Changing Your Baby's Diaper." BabyCenter.com. http://www.babycenter.com/100_guide-to-firsts-first-diaper-change_10350784.bc

6. "Guide to Firsts: Changing Your Baby's Diaper." BabyCenter.com. http://www.babycenter.com/100_guide-to-firsts-first-diaper-change_10350784.bc

7. "SIDS: Reducing Your Baby's Risk." BabyCenter.com. http://www.babycenter.com/baby-sleep-safety

8. "Breastfeeding: Overview." American Pregnancy Association. http://americanpregnancy.org/firstyearoflife/breastfeedingoverview.htm

9. "Benefits of Breastfeeding." Medela.com, 2014. http://www.medelabreastfeedingus.com/benefits-of-breastfeeding

10. Nikole Gipps. "How Do I Prepare My Pet for Our New Baby?" BabyCenter.com, 2014. http://www.babycenter.com/preparing-pets-for-babies

11	Armin Brott. "New Dads: Maintaining Friendships After Baby." BabyCenter.com, 2014. http://www.babycenter.com/0_new-dads-maintaining-friendships-after-baby_8257.bc
12	"Checklist: What to Put in Your Diaper Bag." BabyCenter.com, 2014. http://www.babycenter.com/0_checklist-what-to-put-in-your-diaper-bag_10328766.bc
13	"What Babies Really Cost." Whattoexpect.com, 2014. http://www.whattoexpect.com/preconception/preparing-for-baby/work-and-finance/what-babies-really-cost.aspx
14	"Baby Development, Month by Month." BabyCenter.com, 2014. http://www.babycenter.com/303_baby-development-month-by-month_10380179.bc
15	Emily Bloch. "Baby Poop: A Complete Guide." BabyCenter.com, 2014. http://www.babycenter.com/0_baby-poop-a-complete-guide_10319333.bc
16	"Bathing Your Newborn." BabyCenter.com, 2014. http://www.babycenter.com/0_bathing-your-newborn_1198068.bc
17	Dana Dubinsky. "12 Reasons Babies Cry and How to Soothe Them." BabyCenter.com, 2014. http://www.babycenter.com/0_12-reasons-babies-cry-and-how-to-soothe-them_9790.bc
18	"Colic: What is It?" BabyCenter.com, 2013. http://www.babycenter.com/0_colic-what-is-it_77.bc
19	"Reflux and GERD." BabyCenter.com, 2014. http://www.babycenter.com/0_reflux-and-gerd_10900.bc
20	"When to Call the Doctor for Your Baby." BabyCenter.com, 2014.http://www.babycenter.com/0_when-to-call-the-doctor-for-your-baby_9986.bc
21	"Guide to Firsts: Clipping Your Baby's Nails." BabyCenter.com, 2011. http://www.babycenter.com/100_guide-to-firsts-clipping-your-babys-nails_10348174.bc

22 "Don't Be Surprised by Postpartum Depression." BabyCenter.com, 2014. http://www.babycenter.com/0_dont-be-surprised-by-postpartum-depression_1199780.bc

23 Linton, Bruce. "Five Myths of Fatherhood." BabyCenter.com, 2014. http://www.babycenter.com/0_five-myths-of-fatherhood_8248.bc

24 "Ten Surprises of New Fatherhood." BabyCenter.com, 2014. http://www.babycenter.com/0_ten-surprises-of-new-fatherhood_8253.bc

25 "Collection and Storage of Breastmilk." Medela.com, 2014. http://www.medelabreastfeedingus.com/tips-and-solutions/11/breastmilk-collection-and-storage

26 Spohr, Mike. "19 Things Your Baby Doesn't Actually Need." Buzzfeed.com, 2014. http://www.buzzfeed.com/mikespohr/19-things-your-baby-doesnt-actually-need#10lj7a2

27 "Baby Clothes for the First Six Weeks." BabyCenter.com, 2014. http://www.babycenter.com/0_baby-clothes-for-the-first-six-weeks_519.bc

28 "Baby Development, Month by Month." BabyCenter.com, 2014. http://www.babycenter.com/303_baby-development-month-by-month_10380179.bc

29 "Growth Charts: Taking the Measurements." BabyCenter.com, 2014. http://www.babycenter.com/0_growth-charts-taking-the-measurements_1472623.bc

30 Picoult, Jodi. "Top Tips for Dads on Bonding With Your Baby." BabyCenter.com, 2013. http://www.babycenter.com/0_top-tips-for-dads-on-bonding-with-your-baby_3692.bc

31	"Establishing a Bedtime Routine With Your Baby." BabyCenter.com, 2014. http://www.babycenter.com/0_establishing-a-bedtime-routine-with-your-baby_1507759.bc
32	"Infant Sleep." AskMoxie.org, 2011. http://askmoxie.org/blog/2011/05/infant-sleep.html
33	"Tummy Time: How to Help Your Baby Get Comfortable on his Belly." BabyCenter, 2014. http://www.babycenter.com/0_tummy-time-how-to-help-your-baby-get-comfortable-on-his-bell_1439985.bc
34	Connie Matthiessen. "7 Signs of a Good Doctor." BabyCenter.com, 2014. http://www.babycenter.com/0_7-signs-of-a-good-doctor_10341017.bc
35	"Roseola." KidsHealth.org. The Nemours Foundation, 2012. http://kidshealth.org/parent/infections/skin/roseola.html
36	"Thrush." *Helping Hand*. Nationwide Children's Hospital, n.d. http://kidzdoc.com/wp-content/uploads/2013/12/thrush.pdf
37	"Cradle Cap (Infantile Seborrheic Dermatitis)." KidsHealth.org. The Nemours Foundation, 2011. http://kidshealth.org/parent/infections/skin/cradle_cap.html
38	Armin Brott. Why Communication Breaks Down After Baby and What You Can Do. SheKnows, 2014. http://www.pregnancyandbaby.com/baby/articles/937661/communication-between-new-parents
39	"How to Buy an Infant Car Seat." BabyCenter.com, 2014. http://www.babycenter.com/0_how-to-buy-an-infant-car-seat_5754.bc
40	"How to Buy a Convertible Car Seat." BabyCenter.com, 2014. http://www.babycenter.com/0_how-to-buy-a-convertible-car-

seat_430.bc

41 "Best Toys for Babies." Whattoexpect.com. 21 September 2011. http://www.whattoexpect.com/first-year/photo-gallery/best-toys-for-babies.aspx#/slide-1

42 Tahnk, Jeana Lee. "Top 10 Free Mom Apps." BabyCenter.com, 2014. http://www.babycenter.com/101_top-10-free-mom-apps_10348704.bc

Made in the USA
San Bernardino, CA
12 October 2018